TOMBO

TOMBO

W. S. DI PIERO

MᶜSWEENEY'S
POETRY SERIES

MᶜSWEENEY'S
SAN FRANCISCO

www.mcsweeneys.net

The McSweeney's Poetry Series is edited by Dominic Luxford and Jesse Nathan.

The editors wish to thank assistant editor Rachel Z. Arndt, editorial interns Alison Castleman, Andrew Colarusso, Caroline Crew, Jess Bergman, Neesa Sonoquie, and copyeditor Britta Ameel.

Frontispiece: Paul Klee, *Verfall einer Architektur* (Dilapidation of an architecture), 1938. Pen on paper on cardboard. 11.7 × 8.2 in. Zentrum Paul Klee, Bern © by ARS, New York

ISBN 978-1-938073-76-2

Printed by Thomson-Shore in Michigan.

For Alder

CONTENTS

3.

THE RUNNING DOG

Life, as you say, my friend,
is lived in its transitions.
And there's a yonder
taking place right here.
It lives in the electric air
of field or room,
unseen but palpable
as snow or blowing dust.
A breakfast of poached eggs,
spiked coffee, newsy talk,
crushed sun behind the clouds,
marine layer vapors phasing
blue to green, and the body
quivers through its days
unawares but sensate,
like a dreaming dog
in the still, marbled air
of its own running, the felt
and numb times in between
that are the things around us,
this pigeon feather, acorn,
rinds and grounds and crusts,
any this or that, or words
that pass between us,
while we keep trying to say
here by the stove or on your street
exactly what it's like.

1

STARTING OVER

I can't not keep coming back
to this place that's not a place,
its pepper trees, olive trees, lilac,
narcissus, jasmine, here with me
and mock orange and eucalyptus
and cypress flat-topped by sea wind.
Here are interstate concrete,
desert dust, hardpan,
here are cobblestones
and steep bricky streets,
Death Valley's salt flats,
here red granite domes
that cool at night and groan.
The vagrant imagination
rushes toward the world
in fear of forgetting anything:
witness and invent, it says,
and stay in motion in every
invented place. It tells me,
here you are the nothing
that is this place,
and all places are you,
none of them yours to keep.

SUMMERTIME SUMMERTIME

The foghorns this morning
test tones in the dark.
Or I'm hearing them thus.
A hoarse baritone bellow
laid over reedy swells,
high-toned laments,
a thin, expiring bugle.
And behind them a whisper
of something not quite sound,
a respiration of mist
keeping alive those sounds
I want and need to think
are whales of the deep,
their hymns and carolings
breaking above the waves,
when we sleepers think
in dreams we hear life recede
from the world, beginning
     in the distance,
          in the unlit deep.
             Their song wakes me.

IT'S THAT TIME

The quiet of night hours
isn't really quiet.
You hear the air hiss
even when it doesn't move.
It's a memory of day.
No traffic hushing up
and down tricky hills
among the camphor trees.

No foghorns, no phantoms
shrilling before streetcars
rumble from tunnels.
The absences keep us alert.
No rain or street voices,
nobody calling
*Hannah, you walk the dog
tonight yet or what?*

But there are certain things:
the sexy shifting of trees,
the refrigerator buzzing
while Cherubino sings
the best of love is enthusiasm's
intense abandon, a voice
in song that preys on no one
and is unconscious of its joy.

HAYES STREET EVENING FUGUE

Suppenküche Babies Zonal Citizen Cake
Upstairs: inept blues amped, a silhouette at a drawing board,
a blacked-out window, jeans and socks on a line.
What happens in those rooms? Everybody's a secret
with a secret. The light locks them up. A photo hound
deploys draperies and shades. Looming lingerie
fills with flesh. A woman in pajamas, maybe in love,
sways to sounds only she can hear.
Next door, a baby girl's face, slicked with mucus,
pastes itself to a window while Buxtehude
(who offers Bach his post if he weds the daughter:
Bach says no, oh no) exalts through those rooms,
those organ pipes sounding heaven on earth,
and behind the child's face the mother weaves:
it's Aphrodite, apparitional in the weave,
caretaking those who love and live one story up.

SLEEPING POTIONS

and resulting slushy fugue state meant
  next day I couldn't remember
    writing what I thought I saw:
    a hole among blue spruce, craterous,
not scooped or dug but a vortex plunge
  that appeared as a light switched on
    then dimmed: the light isn't inside it,
  the light is the hole itself, and from within
a tree rises, a screwy trunk and crushed crown,
      and below it clings a nested mass
    of voles, rabbits, scarabs, and wormy matter,
adolescent roots wagging under the tree's abdominals.
  It hovers like an alien ark
    colonizing the mind's eye,
  waiting for, it seems to me, a new world
and its Mirandas. I know, with the dream knowledge
  that chastises reason and makes me
    shake with dread,
    that the seeds now filling the air
like poplar fluff or dust of snow
  are poisons falling into the hole
    while granulated gasses spray
  from the spruce and other viral trees unseen
that wrap around the horizon.

ONE NIGHT AT THE END OF WINTER

The steady rain isn't really steady.
    It ticks my roof,
        hushes, rouses,
    ticks harder, stops,
drags uneven tracks down my windows.
    A storm moon tonight,
        winter's last full moon before
    expectation tips toward spring:
the rains will then be gone,
    the rabbit will be in the moon,
        the windowpanes will
    no longer weep
our opaque eroded selves.
    On such a spring night,
        under these impassive stars,
    on this planet going around our boiled sun:
on such a night the women of my people
    stood outside, opened their purses,
        and yelled to the senseless night,
    with an ain't-it-useless laughter,
Full moon, full moon, fill it up, fill it up!
    Tonight's rain falls in Pisces,
        and our daily want
    secretes hot petitions
while the night, wanting nothing, turns and turns
    as its galaxies in time past and future
        burn, collapse, darken.
    And what of prayers and words

if our universe is one of identical others
that burn with us in time,
and we live this moment
in every other universe?
We and our similars
wish that the rains would end.

WALKING THE DUBOCE TRIANGLE

In autumn, in our western city, at end of day
the sunlight rolls out shadows, the air
brings early dark, we see one lean redbreast
jumping branch to branch, few leaves fall,
there's no frost, a jaybird cuts across our view,
and box-kite strings, and big Blue Angels
that catch burnt reds on disappearing wings.
We look for fallen leaves to kick. We're mortal,
we want more leaves, our seeking saddens us,
our absent autumn waits for us somewhere,
and we can't find the place. Its bite and thrust,
the sting of lastness, its colder air that burns
into our throat, tease us with autumn's absence,
and we hold more tightly to the knowledge of
what's not with us but leaves us anyway.

EARTHQUAKE AND
FOLLOWING TSUNAMI

N-Judah phlegmy with sulky kids,
 wilted adults pale or wind-chapped—
it's St. Patrick's Day, or Gay Pride, any parade
 in raspy Pacific sunshine.
Our commune of bluesy cheer, fried enfolding fathers,
 teenage girls hostage to fortune
wanting children of their own someday,
 and aging mothers who shriek
at the tot staggering toward a handrail,
 holding a balloon he looks to in hope,
fearless when his face crunches against a seat
 and the crowd cries. Nobody hurt. Thank God.
And so he wails and we're wearied by mirth
 and comity and cold pretzels,
westward bound for Ocean Beach.
 The sun roasts the horizon,
blood runners chasing yellow juices.
 I think (and I'm wrong)
that everybody's going home, anticipating home,
 an arrival, a warm housing,
deliverance of their bodies to love and trust.
 I think (and am not wrong)
that love is extravagant hazard, like worse weather
 coming from afar
that blows in unseen and strikes
 while we're charmed by sunset sublimes.

NOCTURNE

Where are you now
my poems,
my sleepwalkers?
No mumbles tonight?
Where are you, thirst,
fever, humming tedium?
The sodium streetlights
burr outside my window,
steadfast, unreachable,
little astonishments
lighting the way uphill.
Where are you now,
when I need you most?
        It's late. I'm old.
              Come soon, you feral cats
                among the dahlias.

2

THE GOLDBERG VARIATIONS

I had to look it up. I thought it was a fish,
not the tail of hair the man you called your boy
swung among the CDs and vintage vinyl bins.
We give our heads away to hair. It takes no time
and smacks of short-term wowies but speaks
imagination's desire for what's complete,
for long love, the Goldberg Variations, a full meal
like burgers a man cooks on a George Foreman
spliced to a power line to feed his roofless pals.
Your mullet could hardly find his way home,
cook beans and rice, or tend, somewhere, his son.
But the mullet is about music, the fullness
of a fearless middle-aged schoolgirl crush,
so forgive me if I thought *There she goes again,*
inviting the bad for the good because of course
we do it all the time, if we live for passion,
the more of things, an aria, burger bliss,
so forgive me for thinking *She knows better,*
she can't really mean 'Maybe he'll change,'
embittered and slammed so many times already
by other youngsters with fades or Hasidic locks,
the one-nighter skinhead, the Mohawk bouncer,
because it's you who use them up, for love:
Can't help it, I even loved that gelled lizardine.

HUB CAP: AN ESSAY ON POETRY

Stingy brims, flip-flops, and guayaberas,
under Prospect Park's sooty trees, late-day
shadows austere on the ground, Dominicans
setting up while ladies in maguey headscarves
hold court behind coolers and beans-and-rice.
Life's lived at its obscure peripheries
except for nuclear ceremonial moments
of Red Stripe, hotlink fumes, graphite laughs.
Jazz Jam plays out like this in summertime
and dying light falls on the congregants,
including the high school kid who shows late.
The elders give him the look. Man-child,
you're sitting in with elders, so listen up:
the solo breath inhales older sounds
so it can make a new noise of its own:
you have to find your way in first before
you find a wired passion all your own.
He unpacks, he buffs, he clears the spit keys.
The indifferent ancients comp and roll
while the kid pinches mouthpiece to embouchure
to crave a sound that blends the dirt and air
and treetops the air washes through.
He plays a lot like Freddie Hubbard, badly,
he flubs the boiled plump sound he's pining for,
he misses time, cracks, winces at clams.
Summer's truth may be he lacks the gift.
The touch might come. He's still too green.

He breaks and looks at the horn as if
the sacramentals that could redeem him
hide inside its bell. Making real music:
you either have it or you don't. The rest
is giving incoherence a restless shape.
His soured, downcast puzzlement says it:
beauty is cruel and makes its dark demands,
it wants what it wants,
               it doesn't forgive,
                    and it ignores us.

BRUISED FRUIT

White

These sun-poached pages like an old address book
I've thumbed and redacted for too many years,
these panting lines too late for consciousness—
I thought they'd give back and refresh life events
I carry like bruised fruit leaking in my shoulder bag.
These scabby practice lines mark where I've been and failed
to give a right voice to scenes, to breakage and joy,
to plain plates of jam and bread, going around not into
life's flash and flesh, trying to complete the world,
as if it needs me to complete it, or give it voice.
The words turn like the leaves of fall then lie
like moths on a sill. As if I could correct life.

Yellow

And blistered legal pads from thirty years ago,
broken-off lines, my homely morose graffiti, contrite,
disfigured, quaintly ringed by morning coffee.
The work is to somehow talk ourselves beyond
the sleepiness of selfhood, to sound out and shape
what's best and worst in us, from fine mindful love
to atrocities that gust across today's reports—
this chalky air, smoke, windblown trash,
flyers and burger wraps and the copybook that leaps
from the wrist of a boy jumping broken glass or puddles
in a charred street that looks not quite like a street,
women in niqabs running, the papers blowing faster.

BOLOGNA 1974

They waved from schoolgirls' panda backpacks
and from women's shopping sacks and frosted hair:
sprigs that weren't from our southern mimosa,
though *mimosa* is what they all called it—
the sweet florets came from the *Acacia fragrans*
which grows in San Francisco, on my street,
where neighbors call all acacias mimosas.
They were sprigs with tiny dandelion florets
that sold all over Italy that day,
cherished even by the surly banana lady
who smiled at me from her street-side booth
small as a Baroque chaise chair but not Baroque,
and the *vigile* directing traffic deranged
by her smile and the blooms behind her ear.
And to women I knew or loved or waited to love
on that March 8th, when those yellow flowers
pass man to woman, woman to woman,
and remember the one hundred and forty-six
of the Shirtwaist Factory fire, dreary facts,
girls trapped behind locked sweatshop doors,
the bodies falling from 9th-floor windows,
the past too urgent and stale at once.
Nobody seemed a stranger to anyone else,

the air was gay and fancy free and I
was five years far from home and walked
for hours past the flowers and their hosts
who hurried and laughed in the chill, stony air,
before spring would deliver us
to ourselves and from memory, again.
That's how it felt at the time.

COPPERS AND GOLDS

Those years, to our child I sang
how far Saint Francis and friends
walked the sheep and goat paths,
shouldering their sacks
like crusty bindlestiffs
who hoboed Ohio to Kansas,
steel mills to prairie wheat,
bad shoes and stomachs
that bitched righteously
at starchy barons back home.

     Still walking,
          hungry still,
Market Street's evangels,
gleaners, pissy backpacks,
druggy lamentations
in winter's late, low light
metallic like the copper floods
that lit Bologna's porticos
the night we varoomed into town
before our daughter was born,
reckless with laughter and youth
before love became habit's slug.

The years go.
        More stage-lit cities.
Tungsten, travertine, brass.
More hushed, faraway rooms,
the heart's icy ache
before meaty Dutch double
portraits of the happily wed—
rosy cheeks loyal and true,
love's habits excited, renewed
in each other's sight. O child grown,
we're lost to the fast fires
of time, and enthralled.
Recall that song's sweetest line:
Dice al fuoco, sei il mio fratello.

OYSTERCATCHERS AND LOVERS

1.

My marshy night drains into day.
I'm remembering a greasy photo
from a seaside honky-tonk:
a common murre half-swallowed
by a sea anemone:
the bird's a fat man stuck
in a hairy chimney,
the anemone's raunchy
come-to-me maw
droll, famished, thoughtless.

2.

Things happen all at once
but I can't write it down:
the estuarial plenitude
of pelicans, cattails, catkins,
oystercatchers on rocks,
one and one and one,
and tide pool ribs that file out
to sea like broken, train-set
skyscrapers on shriveled avenues
in our lost cities. Now what?

3.

Now I'm in my city, in the Mission: I see
teen lovers slouched into each other
like bums sharing a smoke. They hug
through parka pockets and remind me
of two other lovers last night
in Dolores Park. Orange street-cones
blazed soccer goalposts on the grass.
I felt sick with the too-much of it:
my vertigo stood the field on end—
the plush lights, the washed woven greenness.

4.

My scenes are liquids poured into a shadowy me.
The Invisible Man Returns. They tint my blood.
All my Mission lovers darken against cedars
that rotate into view beside the soccer field.
If I go numb to our surround, my love,
press your nails into my palm, I'll do the same
for you, we'll wake each other, again,
to ourselves and the heart's homeless desire
to claim whatever's under the close, dark sky
whited by nebular street-lamp light.

THE BLACK PAINTINGS: THE MOUTH

The kisser, the drooler, the sucker,
the crooked overbite
sexing up an upper lip,
puce ulcers puffing
a lower lip and cracked
tablature of teeth,
a place for the tongue
to lie in rest, in wait.
We greet reality with
a one-way-or-the-other
mouth, like the homeless
cankered face on my corner
grinning for change
for coffee, or that kid's
snotty wired smile,
or my next door neighbor's
felonious gold incisor.
Goya's mouths are sites
of being, fouled canals,
rain rushing gutters to flush
slops and excrement aglitter
with nervous lusts,
angers, hungers, grubs
foraging life's ruins and offal
essential to damnation and glee.

THE MENDICANTS

Leave me alone. Be abject elsewhere.
        Don't wait at night outside my door,
              all of you I've loved,
          shivering, wanting in, O my friends,
blood relations, nobodies, anybodies,
        who beg for lines like these,
                who grab and squeeze my arm
          and tell me to testify here
to trouble, joy, the juicy, the dry.
        What more can you want?
                I give back what I can,
          unfinished sounds half heard,
a changing shape of smoke or spit.

INJUN JOE AS AN AVATAR

The poetry's arrested in Joe's scene,
which can't be trusted, because I saw it
through painkillers that softened my head
after I'd asked him what Keats really meant:
"Was it a vision, or a waking dream?"
—*You think that really mattered much to him?*
In my waking dream, there's no glory,
no prize committee or dew-drip Paradise.
He's in an attic, or a dim garage,
or the cellar where he actually writes,
the space a sheeted granulated matter,
his silenced countenance and de-boned body
scabby with caked ash about to crust and crack,
poems piled at his feet like shoeshine rags.
A grave purpled fraughtness colors him.
What damaged him to this silence?
He still writes and still isn't heard, as if
not being heard is the whole point,
and who are these children, these waving
Halloween windsocks who won't talk to him?
Beyond my busybody vision, he staggers
through divorce, stooped, bereft, still writing.
Spiky and singing, he out-writes them all,
the cheered, spotless others—he howls
at their after-dinner poetry,
the monsignors, the suburbans, the woo-woo
wisdom merchants weeping to the bank.
Poetry's a storm outside a cellar,
sunshine at a bedroom window.

Too much schoolroom poisons the idiom.
Too much reverence stinks up the joint.
The sorrow hanging in the dreamy air
confuses him, he can't understand
how his heart came to hurt him like this,
confuses it with leaves in a storm, the leaves
of the poems that keep falling
in the cellar, the base desires and rage—
he says the gods designed the set,
stage manage things, scripted them,
and the hilarity that hurts us
is that none of it really matters,
that poetry's griefs are intimates
            we don't choose.
                  They come to us, for us.
      They cling to body and soul.

LATE LESSONS

The ghost in the music is its sheerest music,
late nights, the house and its humans asleep,
mayflies and spiders inquiring at the screen.
The stool, wilted pages, instrument opened
to a screech owl keyed-up for field mice.
Or when everybody's out, prairie dust
wedging the windows, her aging hands
raw from lye-soap pick across
childhood's plinky, broken scales—
Vienna to stateside, Strauss to Tulsa,
she practices, like dampened prayer,
only when no one can hear her play.

And now her years come down to you,
to crumbling land's end and its tides,
her piano's badly tuned voice
groggy, down to your nervous nights
while fog strains through the garden gate.
Loose keys, lost motion, muddy chords:
they're yours, they listen back at you.
When will you override what's imperfect
and simply play? When is the timing right
to practice your dozen remembered things?
Your family is sleeping now.
They won't hear you make mistakes.

THE SMELL OF SPEARMINT

He told, he didn't suggest or ask.
So when the unfinished father
told the son to do it, the son obeyed
and laid out razor and Barbasol
next to the bed-tray's plastic cups,
ashtray, straws, and mucilage
of scrambled eggs. Forty-three,
he demanded to look clean and spare.
We die with habits of self-regard.
The son, seventeen, can't know
that when he's his father's age,
a life's love would soap his face,
run the blade, nick a nostril
—*hold still, you nervous you*—
then pass into time's menthol airs.
He trowels, plumps, pats the lather,
he turns the head, he drags the trucky
brutish double-blade down
jaw and hollowed cheeks:
it planes the meaty manly whiskers,
it resists its task, yet life feels lighter
in his hand, most of all when it lies
lightly on the cabled throat.
One big bone, the father's head,
in custody of the speechless son,
the untrained hand that never knew
the contents of that bone, does what
it's told to do, and can't know
what love will bring back in time.

3

OTHER WAYS TO HEAVEN

The unspeakable beauty of facts,
their acts and scenes, the trapeze flier
flipping toward the catcher across our gasp,
trolley contact rods that bow from catenaries
cresting a hill before the bulky ahnnn appears—
systemic pleasures, a little off but actual,
that make us feel at home in our elusive lives.

A husband slices morning toast. The wife,
still asleep, wanders among secrets scratched
like starlines in the skull's hysterical heavens.
And hillside windows at dawn, watered gold,
like consciousness waking, filling up with time.
Rivers pokey in April snow, torrential now,
rising under our feet.
                              These aren't illustrations,
they happen, more hours pass. A sea-blown
summer wind hums through the window harp
across your face, a book drowsy in your hands,
an ecstasy of presence, the sweet, the sour,
motions in the wind being only what they are.

Wait and watch. Wood smoke atomizes birches,
coons tip over garbage cans, fog bumps
casements years have rattled loose,
hedgerow shadows shift like heads and hair
of children rising from bed whose shadows
move like dark clouds on their walls,
their voices coming awake like rain,

or the creaky arbor ladder your neighbor climbs
to string Christmas lights in mock oranges
that bloom so sweet in spring and hold
this turning, still-fresh set of last night's stars.

IMAGINATION RUNNING AWAY

Stars our needy selves once thought were gods
that we've re-imagined into excited gasses,
carbon, boiled airs, uneternal embers . . .
They're looking down, though we know
they're not really looking: you and I,
like children on our backs on fresh-cut grass,
while canister freight cars roll through town
like heaven's bull-roarers. What did those gods see?
Ether oceans, green deserts, soiled spines and ribs,
and deep in our nappy bush they see us now,
hopeful watchers listening, as if for music
of the spheres, glassy choirs heard so long
but never really heard. Yet we watchers wait,
measure our lives by such hope, these ardent
liquid lights propagating more of their kind,
huger than time, though what can be so?
We're here, we wait for a voice, a shared song,
a stellar hum like orchard bees, something
more than our own clingy words,
a voicing that we also know won't come,
not tonight, while we lie here living out
our starry-night desire, and know again
      how small it is,
           this human largeness
              we believe ourselves to be.

QUE TAL

I'm in this bright café,
its yellow tropical air:
a green plaster toucan,
potted palm, skulls
in thrall to laptop screens,
when some bereavement,
sourceless and angular,
visits my idle heart.
Lovers look away
from one another,
some smile into phones,
the unworldly service girl
wipes the food-case glass
and slides doilies around.
It's so unbecoming
to receive it here.
The chalkboard preaches plenty,
a fountain pours from
a jaguar's jaws to stone,
I ask its constant motion
to carry me through the hour's
heaviness and the rain outside
to my bathroom mirror,
my humid flesh, my face,
its pouchings and matchtip scars.

Let me be fool enough
to read meaning into
the twiggy lightning that cracks
the darkening distance,
such meaning as animals
like me need to see.

BLUE MONDAY

The years turn blue.
Hours badly lit,
a flybuzz fluorescence
of hospital corridor,
a South Side dive's
sulky blues-harp airs.
Blue in the face,
I canal the streets,
one becomes another,
my scenes stare back.
Early morning sweepers
on Rome's sultry ways,
brooms like scythes
harvesting trash
while sewer crews rake
leaf gunk from gutters.
The Calabrian cobbler dwarf
loathes my request
to stretch a shoe,
then withdraws into
bench-room darkness,
and in a different city's
subway passage through
glassed-in Etruscan roads
another artisan says sure
I can stretch the fit,
and two pirogues cut
a flooded Louisiana avenue.

And with all these,
in the same space
time composes,
Pacific light fades
behind orange headlands,
a coyote crosses
Golden Gate Bridge
in summer's drippy fog,
a burnt orange stripe
lights the horizon behind
Monument Valley's buttes
and their sea-trench shadows.
Third Avenue cabs bristle
through a summer drizzle,
crows toss their floppy ash
over Michigan Avenue,
and ravens on my street
sing songs that poets envy,
between rain's windowpanes
and the gray blue sea.

POEM WITH AN ALTERED LINE BY
FREDERICK TUCKERMAN

I'll try to make this simple. Two nights, same dream.
Wind-chimed by the fraught owlish emptiness
you expect in small, dry towns, cinders and dust
smack the air, and raw material demands
the freight train run on time every night.
Javelinas pick on prickly pear while
I count a great-horned owl, jackrabbits,
and gray fox like the kit that walked onto
the balcony of that winged new house,
where the landscape architect showed us dozens
of native plants, especially the fan-dancers,
those species of intoxicating sage
we stuffed in flutes and pitchers like greetings—
but I'm complexifying, as usual,
saying what should be simply something said,
and at any rate this is really about the train.
In that high-desert west Texas town
where the old movie house is a realtor's suite
and the thrift-shop's grouchy wind-vane coot
pecks small change from a sewing box,
every night (I'm getting to the dream)
the long long train rants right through town,
roars a green soapy air tingled with dirt,
our bodies safe and compact in bed,
warmed by summer. Desiccated streetlamps,
boxcars, hoppers, flatbeds, tank cars. Real,
all of this, and my dream was as real as that,
then next night it came again the same,

and you again were somehow there with me.
I still can't rid the scene or hold it close,
the two of us stood there, outside time,
neither of us going anywhere:
the crossing lights, the train, its graveled sound,
its headlamp beaming on our lost world.
Why do I love that lonely scene so much?

WHAT'S LEFT

How often now, raging weeping for the days
love gives then takes away, takes from you
the slightly chapped hand laid on the one
you're pointing at a tree, and the voice
that breathes *coffeeberry bush* into your mouth.

The finger that taps and feathers your ear
but the giggle's gone before you turn around.
The sandalwood scent hanging in the room,
the auburn strand like a flaw in the porcelain,
the nail clipping's sting in the carpet.

The days eat into your stomach, bite you
with longing for relief from love
that you cannot leave or leave alone,
from its trashy fires where you won't
burn down to ash or be transformed.
You become them, and they keep burning,
and they have a *coffeeberry* voice.

THE HORIZON LINE

I spoke not of Campana's woman
of Genova, who brought him seaweed
in her hair, and sea wind on her skin—
your curls swung wet and whippy,
the surf took over your ankles
and knocky knees, your hair opened,
the tide calmed, and the farther you swam
the more you were sun-cuts on the sea
and I panicked to lose sight of you,
less than a dashed shadow disintegrating
into opaque radiance where sea and sky
shrink to a seam of life continuous
with our own. In your own good time
you brought back wind in your hair,
her hair, seaweed smelly, hot,
wind shot with salt and seaweed
dripping from that hair, as if
such disappearance and return
were your nature. When you flopped
on our fleecy blanket,
      tart water seeds
           popped from your hair.
               I tasted them.

SO IT GOES

That marsh hawk,
its blown-leaf flight
through Tomales Bay fog,
summer's abraded light,
the Pacific tide pressuring
and pinching wave on wave
into the bay's inlet . . .
We feel somehow between us
still water crushed by that sea
so constant it seems not to be.
The hawk tumbles, stops,
stands on the air,
fans its wings as if to shoo
the sun's drenched veils,
and its treading wings stop
our unstoppable argument
that love goes, who knows why,
and delivers us from pain
to pain, air with teeth
that seems to eat more air.
Owlish northern harrier,
who listens with your face
and shows not love but want,
speed, life in flight
toward, only toward,

pausing at every chance
to use what ocean-born
bayside air sustains
by resisting. We thank
your sunken head bones
and wild close-to-water seeking
that somehow speaks to us,
delivers us
to another amazed
agonized place.

THERE WERE SUCH THINGS

I knew the words would be waiting for me,
how sounds play in the mouth and mind,
each time a different estero in my heart
    your bracelet's lost coral scale
      your broken hairpin
    the lipstick smudge
      sliding off torn tissue
an event each time, thing by thing,
word by word. I knew these creatures, as before,
would be waiting in their lovely names,
in *dowitcher willet whimbrel coot*
or *snipe* or *curlew*, that I could speak and speak.
    Where were you that day?
    Why weren't you with me?
What waited there was something else.
Muscling nonstop around each other,
dingy leopard sharks shadowed
the shallows, light dying on their backs.
They seemed to be themselves the moving waters.
They were the swimming absence of the words
they drove away, part of the new vocabulary
of exclusions, of what might have been birds.

THE BIRDS OF THE AIR

The Cooper's I now see farther down trail
pulls my vision to red-tail mates dialing
through blues above a sparrowhawk's crown
that turns from phone lines toward elk cows
bugling near the heron hunting gophers—
the just enough always too much already.
This coastal track we followed years ago
poppies redwoods fiddleheads monkeyflower
mistletoe oh the healing mistletoe
that clings to the live oaks it falls from
while we agreed we could not be as we were
and wind rushed through our ears our voices
as it's rushing now as if our voices still say
no this can't be what we meant or wanted.
How many times we said that. It must have been
what we wanted talking so much helplessly
about what's not here anymore is its own kind
of plenitude, isn't it? How lucky are we.

THE BIG BEACH BOOK

The painted lady you teased you wouldn't free
clapped from your hands into the stiff beach wind
and joined its thousand similars: pages flew loose
from that loafy book you'd brought because
an old flame teased you'd never crack its French.
You slapped at them the way you once beat flames
that grease-arced jet to pan to towel, while guilt
dragged you through decrepit pages until
they flew and flocked among the butterflies
when, remotely hand in hand, through the dunes
we walked back to the car, laughing at your r's.
I drove too fast, failed again to watch,
to see us later, at the end of things,
when all this, like us, would go.
The butterflies swiped our view, we lost our way,
we took our eyes off the road, we broke through
their dense flight, ecstatic separately.

THE HEART

The estero swells
with winter rain.
We run toward
not away from
stress and trouble.
We want to get closer
to the rising waters,
wait and watch them
flush from and back to
the terrifying ocean.
Nothing comes from
nothing. No. Everything
comes from everything.
The heavy clouds
settle on the hills,
an egret's cry peels
through thick wind,
cattails lean landward.
We're aroused by our
small, dimming world.
We say we smell
salt and seaweed
even when we don't.
Those cattails bend
away from the wind.
Be constant in
inconstancy, love,
be the kingfisher
flying from the wire.

AS IT WERE UPON THE TONGUE
(OR WHO ATE THE JAM?)

1.

Breakfast again, like the one once here
with that one he lost—we become so lost
in the sorry whiteness of our kitchens,
and like children lost in a monstrous wood,
we panic. It's too hard to find our way.
There is no way. Acid overnight coffee,
fig jam, her star-flecked pajama bottoms'
flannel firmament, her bed-messed hair
like unlicked wings. We must forget these things.
We who don't forget to fantasticate
what shepherds and star-gazing seekers left
to parents in rags and glamorous child.
There are worse moments, no lack among
ruined people peopling our ruined planet.

2.

So (again) here sits the depleted man
at breakfast, with fig jam Griffino made,
crushed from fruit G.'s flyboy father planted,
after shooting down *mucho* MIGs, hotshot
sky king who, for love, slammed his loving son
not against the adolescent trees
whose leaves fanned flies from the child's eager face,

but against the cowboys on his bedroom wall
and its happy horses during happy hour.
The depleted man spreads the Christmas jam,
recalls the teeth of she who ate the seeds
while Baghdad's bombs jumped from the radio.
Unasked-for gift. Fey cowboys on the wall.
How compare anyone's loss to someone else's?

3.

We lack world-love, and mercy. Why do we
turn from joy? Helpless love aspires to taste
heaven while eating dirt. This is our way.
In fig leaves we read winter's short lifelines.
The imagination craves what heavens have.
He sees the planets reabsorbed by sun.
It is the way for we who weep for lost love,
lost things, sorrowing things, ring, eyelash, figs,
on subways, in mangers, in darkened orchards,
who taste the seedy rub against the tongue
that once in winter touched another's tongue,
O sweet preserves, O raspy, tickly fruit
once fresh, brandied, simmered, now spread upon
this stale, isolate, day-after-Christmas bread.

THE ASH BRINGER

A grainy predawn dark, expressway traffic
pulling arterial tail-lights across gray water
and its blue heart. Under Lemon Hill,
grunts from Boathouse Row, woodshed clunks,
young men's voices too loud for a day
expanding into starless skies—bad boys
hungover after keg night push long sculls
into the water and slice its marcelled run,
a marbled wake behind each silenced stroke
and coxswain counting that muscled steadiness
past the Water Works, Spring Garden Street Bridge,
and Girard Avenue Bridge, where on the bank
Eakins sketches Max Schmitt in a single scull,
his tinfoil light like this, where the crews sweat off
last night's lost time but won't row way far north
to river canals, Manayunk Reach, its towpath,
mules and barges and anthracite from Point Carbon
to feed stoves and Bessemers in Harrisburg, Pittsburgh . . .
Downriver, behind the boats and finny tracks,
League Island, where cheats and pimply teens parked
and tricked fingers through nipple hairs, satiny tufts,
the shut-down Navy Yard, once staggering shore leave
for so many thousands dead, how many more since,
in the rivers, of the rivers, like the girl
at a bend near the museum gazebo: she tips
a throe of ashes from a brassy urn,
kneeling, not pious, just there, slanting her head
as if to speak to the passing, do it right,

shrug fine ores into the river—it takes so long
to cast away so little left of kin or friend
to Schuylkill, Delaware, Chesapeake, Atlantic,
someone she knew, walked gardens with, and must have loved.

TOMBO

In Safeway yesterday, a young man sat on the floor,
     pulled off his shoes, granted audience to us,
his fellow seekers, and picked his naked feet.
     He smiled, our brother, at the story he told
of deliverance at the hand of Master Tombo,
     lord and creator, whose round energy
lives in us surrounds us surrounds our milk
     our butter our eggs: see Him there,
in the slurpee glaze upon the freezer case?
     In that elder by the yoghurt shelves?
I believed his happiness, and coveted
     a tidy universe. He picked his feet
while a child whimpered by the melons, her nanny's
     mango aura made the cold blown air
touch my brain, I smelled myself in my aging body
     and felt my silly bones collapse again.
I wanted Tombo's dispensation to save
     this faint believer and the indifferent world
that rivers through and past me. Down my aisle
     lavender respired from the flower stall
and Security spoke kind words to our prophet.
     Oh I love and hate the fickle messy wash
of speech and flowers and winds and tides,
     and crave plain rotund stories
to justify our continuity. To the Maya, corn was god,
     spilled blood made corn grow,
the blood gods shed watered needy ground
     and became People who worshipped the corn.

Tombo's grace can carry us, convinced, from one
        inarticulate incoherent moment to the next.
Tonight the wet streets and their limelight sigh.
        Orion on fire turns, unchanged again.
Bread rises somewhere and its ovens scent the trees.
        My poor belief lives in the only and all
of the slur of what these are, and what these are
        streams toward loss in moments we live through.
As children we were lost in our opaque acts
        but fresh and full in time. I remember
how I touched a girlish knee, how one boy
        broke another's face, how we all stood
in hard gray summer rain so it would run
        down the tips of noses to our tongues.

ACKNOWLEDGMENTS

Many of these poems first appeared in the following magazines: *Poetry, Threepenny Review, Orion, California Northern, Zyzzyva, Mānoa,* and *Plume.*

*   *   *

Two poems are dedicated to old friends and like travelers: "The Running Dog" goes to Christian Wiman, "Injun Joe as an Avatar" to J.T. Barbarese.

"The Smell of Spearmint" goes to the memory of Joseph Di Piero, "As It Were Upon the Tongue" to that of Griffin Fariello. "The Birds of the Air" goes to Mary Jane Di Piero, "Late Lessons" to Jennifer Foerster, "The Goldberg Variations" to Belinda Cooper.

My thanks to Jesse Nathan, for his care and close attention. And to David Breskin, who helped more than anyone to make this book this book.

ABOUT THE AUTHOR

W. S. Di Piero, winner of the 2012 Ruth Lilly Poetry Prize, is the author of ten books of poetry. His poems appear frequently in *Poetry* and *Threepenny Review*, and he has written for the *New York Times Magazine*, the *New York Times Book Review*, the *New Republic*, and many other periodicals. He writes a monthly column on the visual arts for an independent newsweekly, the *San Diego Reader*, and he's a well-known essayist on art, literature, culture, and personal experience. The latest of his five essay collections— *When Can I See You Again?*—contains his recent art writings. Di Piero's autobiographical writings have appeared twice in *Best American Essays*, and he's an accomplished translator of Greek and Italian poetry. He's won a Guggenheim Fellowship, a National Endowment for the Arts grant, and a Lila Wallace-*Readers Digest* Award. Di Piero lives in San Francisco.

THE McSWEENEY'S POETRY SERIES

THE
MᶜSWEENEY'S POETRY SERIES

The McSweeney's Poetry Series is founded on the idea that good poems can come in any style or form, by poets of any age anywhere. Our goal is to publish the best, most vital work we can find, regardless of pedigree. We're after poems that move, provoke, inspire, delight—poems that tear a hole in the sky. And when we find them, we'll publish them the only way we know how: in beautiful hardbacks, with original artwork on the cover. These are books to own, books to cherish, books to loan to friends only in rare circumstances.

>>>—<<<

SUBSCRIPTIONS

The McSweeney's Poetry Series subscription includes our next four books for only $40—an average of $10 per book—delivered to your door, shipping included. You can sign up at store.mcsweeneys.net

>>>—<<<

PREVIOUS TITLES

Fragile Acts by Allan Peterson
"Like 'Brazil's undiscovered caverns of amethyst,' Allan Peterson's *Fragile Acts* is a major find."
—John Ashbery

City of Rivers by Zubair Ahmed
"When reading Zubair Ahmed I feel as though I am both witnessing and taking part in an ecstatic, lyric experience."
—Matthew Dickman

x by Dan Chelotti
"Dan Chelotti's poems spin and jump through fire landing on their feet ... a poet with grace and beauty in his duffle bag."
—James Tate

The Boss by Victoria Chang
"*The Boss* is essential reading for anyone who has ever had a job, a child, a parent, or a heart."
—G. C. Waldrep